INTRODUCTION

This volume contains the airs of some of the most popular English folk-dances.

The tunes are all printed in the keys in which they are published in the pianoforte settings, and certain tunes are printed a second time in a different key. These transpositions have been made for the benefit of players of instruments on which it is difficult, or impossible, to produce a complete range of semitones.

The choice of transposed keys has been determined mainly by the requirements of instruments belonging to the whistle family. The ordinary " tin " whistle plays a major scale of two octaves, but for indoor playing its effective range is limited to an octave, or an octave and a half. For example, in a whistle in the key of D, where the full compass is d' to d''', the most effective range will be from about f♯' to b'', the notes below f♯' being rather too soft for folk-dance accompanying and those above b'' being too shrill. The tunes have therefore, where necessary, been transposed into keys which bring them as far as possible within the compass of f♯' to b''.

In order that whistle players may easily acquire a co-ordination between sight and fingering, they are advised to read D as the bottom keynote of the six- or seven-hole pipe, and G as the bottom keynote of the three- or four-hole pipe, no matter what the actual pitch of the pipe may be. The desired pitch may then be secured by using a pipe of the appropriate length.

The essential elements of folk-dance accompanying are steady time, marked rhythm, and nicety of phrasing.

The phrase marks are reproduced from the pianoforte settings and will be found helpful by those who are reading at sight. Players who are familiar with the melodies may, of course, allow themselves some latitude and may vary the phrasing according to the figures of the dance. The phrase marks should on no account be regarded as slurs. Generally speaking, a smooth legato style of playing is not suited to folk-dance accompanying, and the notes should mostly be detached by tonguing or by separate bowing.

Metronome marks are given only in those cases where there is traditional authority : but the tempo should in no case be regarded as rigidly fixed.

Unless otherwise stated the tune is repeated *ad lib.*

A Selection of

100 ENGLISH FOLK DANCE AIRS

FOR MELODIC INSTRUMENTS

Edited by

MAUD KARPELES

AND

KENWORTHY SCHOFIELD

Originally Published by

THE ENGLISH FOLK DANCE AND SONG SOCIETY, LONDON

(1951)

Hargail Music Press, 28 West 38th St., New York, N. Y. 10018

INDEX

NOTE.—The transpositions can be played to sound in the keys of the pianoforte settings by using a six- or seven-hole pipe in C, or a four-hole pipe in F, for the tunes on pages marked *; and a six- or seven-hole pipe in E, or a four-hole pipe in A, for the tunes on pages marked †.

INDEX—*continued*

CONTENTS

Tunes printed in the same key as the pianoforte version.

COUNTRY DANCES

CONTENTS—*continued*

CONTENTS—*continued*

Tunes printed in transposed Keys:

CONTENTS—*continued*

The books referred to in the Contents are as follows:

COUNTRY DANCES: *The Country Dance Book*, Sets 1-11, by Cecil Sharp (Novello); *Twelve Traditional Country Dances*, by Maud Karpeles (The English Folk Dance and Song Society); *Five Popular Country Dances* (The English Folk Dance and Song Society); *The Country Dance Book*, New Series, No. 1, by Douglas and Helen Kennedy (The English Folk Dance and Song Society); *The Apted Book of Country Dances*, by W. S. Porter, M. Heffer, and A. B. Heffer (W. Heffer & Sons).

RUNNING SET: *The Country Dance Book*, Set 9 (Novello).

SWORD DANCES: *The Sword Dances of Northern England*, Sets 1-3, by Cecil Sharp (Novello).

MORRIS DANCES: *The Morris Dance Book*, Sets 1-10, by Cecil Sharp (Novello).

GALOPEDE

RIBBON DANCE

THE BUTTERFLY

WE WON'T GO HOME TILL MORNING

THE FLOWERS OF EDINBURGH

NANCY'S FANCY

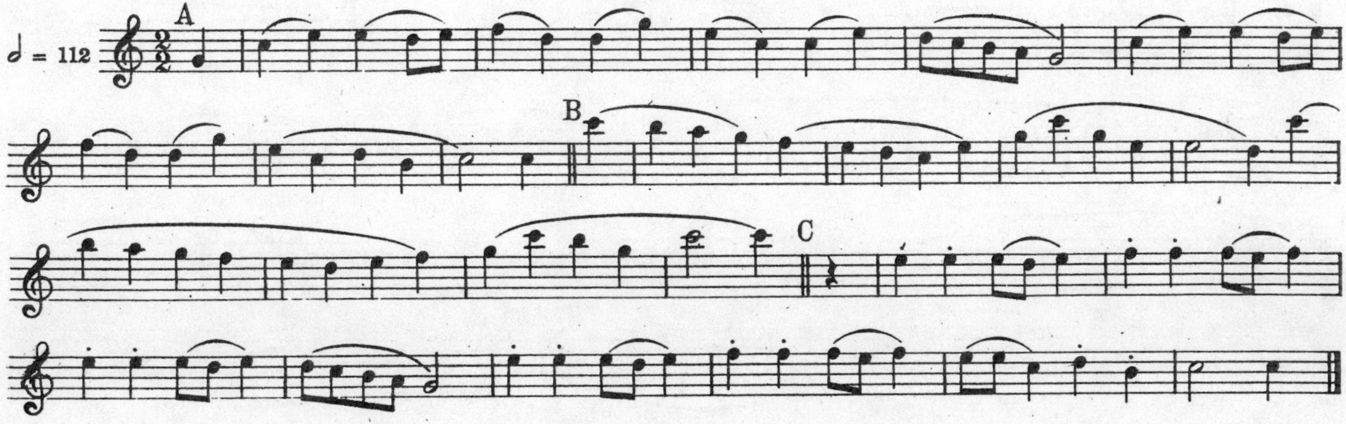

POP GOES THE WEASEL

BONNETS SO BLUE

THE TRIUMPH

HASTE TO THE WEDDING

THREE MEET
or
THE PLEASURES OF THE TOWN

MORPETH RANT

SOLDIER'S JOY

ROXBURGH CASTLE*

*This tune can also be used as an accompaniment to "The Fool's Jig"

THE LONG EIGHT

To the tune of "Haste to the Wedding"

PIPER'S FANCY

To the tune of "The New Rigged Ship"

DURHAM REEL

To the tune of "A Hundred Pipers"

THE TWIN SISTERS

CIRCASSIAN CIRCLE

To the tune of "The Irish Washerwoman"

A1 & 2

This tune is also suitable as an accompaniment to the Rapper Sword Dance.

JENNY PLUCK PEARS

Play 3 times

A1 & 2

MAGE ON A CREE

Play 3 times (with repeat)

A1 & 2

THE FINE COMPANION

NEWCASTLE

ORANGES AND LEMONS

GATHERING PEASCODS

RUFTY TUFTY

PARSON'S FAREWELL

Play 3 times

no ornamentation, please - simple

HEY, BOYS, UP GO WE

Play 3 times

Play this lightly
Breathe it
Crisp
bowing
clear
frog

Break it into 2 notes
Don't hold too long

THE BLACK NAG

Play 3 times

NONESUCH
or
A LA MODE DE FRANCE

GODDESSES

BLACK JACK

JAMAICA

THE TWENTY-NINTH OF MAY

Play 12 times

IF ALL THE WORLD WERE PAPER

Play 3 times

HUNSDON HOUSE

Play 4 times (i.e. 3 repeats)

Play 4 times

CONFESS

THE OLD MOLE

Play 22 times

BROOM, THE BONNY, BONNY BROOM

Play 12 times

THE MERRY, MERRY MILKMAIDS

Play 3 times

OAKEN LEAVES

To the tune of "Touch and Take"

Play 18 times

SELLENGER'S ROUND
or
THE BEGINNING OF THE WORLD

Play 5 times

HIT AND MISS

To the tune of "Daphne"

Play 3 times

THE BOATMAN

Play 3 times

PICKING UP STICKS

To the tune of "Lavena"

Play 17 times

SCOTCH CAP

Play 3 times

MY LADY WINWOOD'S MAGGOT*

To the tune of "Nobody's Jig"

*This tune can also be used as an alternative accompaniment to the Flamborough Sword Dance

CHRISTCHURCH BELLS

THE MOCK HOBBY HORSE

MAID'S MORRIS

SAGE LEAF

* This section, i.e. B, C and D (with repeats), is played as many times as there are couples.

EPPING FOREST

THE MAID IN THE MOON

To the tune of "All in a Garden Green"

Play 3 times

THE MAID PEEPED OUT AT THE WINDOW

or

THE FRIAR IN THE WELL

Play 3 times

CHILDGROVE

INDIAN QUEEN

GREENWICH PARK

JACK'S MAGGOT

APLEY HOUSE

THE GEUD MAN OF BALLANGIGH

To the tune of "Hunt the Squirrel"

THE WAY TO NORWICH

A TRIP TO PARIS

THE FIRST OF APRIL*

*Published by kind permission of Mr. W. S. Porter

THE DRESSED SHIP*

THE SPANIARD*

*Published by kind permission of Mr. W. S. Porter

BARRACK HILL

BUNG YOUR EYE*

This tune must be transposed up one tone if played on the 3 hole pipe.

THE GOOSEBERRY BLOSSOMS

THE BANKS OF ALLAN*

*This tune is also suitable as an accompaniment to Rapper Sword Dances.

MELANCHOLY MARTIN*

*This tune can be used as an alternative accompaniment to the Hey in the Flamborough Sword Dance.

KIRKBY MALZEARD
(THE GIRL I LEFT BEHIND ME)

SLEIGHTS SWORD DANCE

First Figure

BOBBY SHAFTOE

Second Figure

THE COBBLER'S JIG

Third Figure

THREE JOLLY SHEEPSKINS

SLEIGHTS SWORD DANCE

Fourth Figure
BOYNE WATER

NO MAN'S JIG

FLAMBOROUGH SWORD DANCE

THREE JOLLY SHEEPSKINS

𝅗𝅥 = 104

THE STAFFORDSHIRE HORNPIPE

𝅗𝅥 = 104

RAPPER SWORD DANCE*

THE COUNTRY COURTSHIP

HANDSWORTH SWORD DANCE

THE GIRL I LEFT BEHIND ME

*Other tunes suitable for Rapper Sword Dances are "Bung your Eye" and "The Banks of Allan," see page 26, and "The Irish Washerwoman," see page 10.

ASKHAM RICHARD SWORD DANCE

THE FISHER LADDIE

ASKHAM RICHARD SWORD DANCE

BOBBY SHAFTCE

BEAN SETTING

COUNTRY GARDENS

Introduction (4 bars). Then play twice.

RIGS O' MARLOW

Introduction (4 bars). Then play 4 times.

TIDESWELL PROCESSIONAL MORRIS

Introduction (4 bars). Then repeat ad libitum.

BLUE-EYED STRANGER

Introduction (4 bars). Then play 4 times.

JOCKIE TO THE FAIR

Introduction (8 bars).

OLD MOTHER OXFORD

SHEPHERDS' HEY
HEADINGTON JIG

Introduction (4 bars). Then play 4 times; and A music, a fifth time.

BACCA PIPES JIG
To the tune of "Green Sleeves"
(First Figure)

Introduction (8 bars). Then play 4 times; and A music, a fifth time.

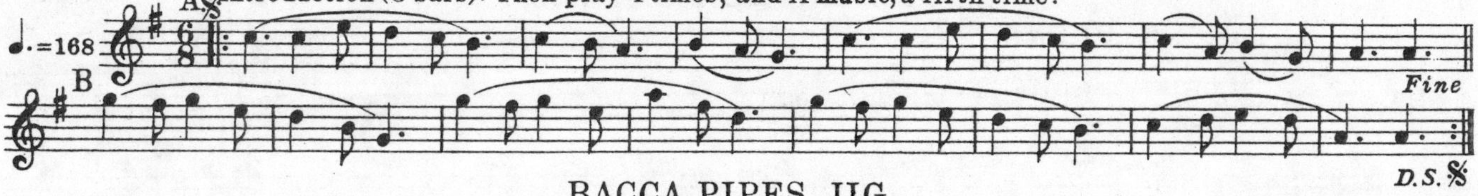

BACCA PIPES JIG
(Fourth Figure)

Introduction (8 bars). Then play 4 times; and A music, a fifth time.

CONSTANT BILLY
ADDERBURY

LADS A BUNCHUM
ADDERBURY

GLORISHEARS
BAMPTON

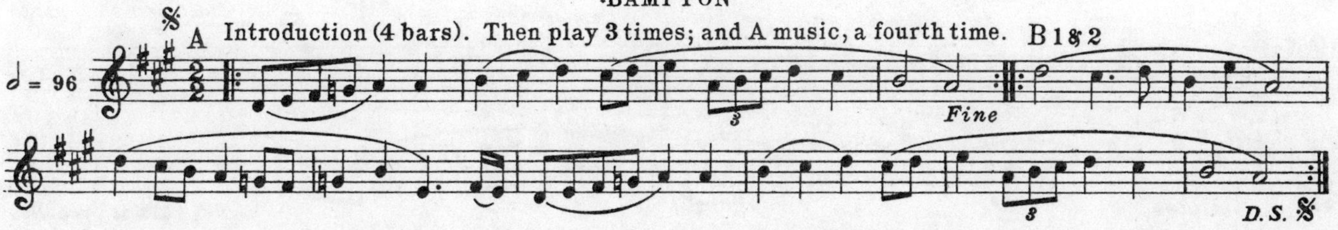

BONNY GREEN GARTERS

JOCKIE TO THE FAIR

BRACKLEY

STEP BACK

Introduction (8 bars). Then play 3 times; and A music, a fourth time.

LADIES' PLEASURE

Introduction (8 bars). Then play A.B.C. B.C.B.

HELSTON FURRY DANCE

Introduction (4 bars). Then play ad lib.

THE BUTTERFLY

NANCY'S FANCY

BONNETS SO BLUE

HASTE TO THE WEDDING

SOLDIER'S JOY

ROXBURGH CASTLE*

*This tune can also be used as an accompaniment to "The Fool's Jig"

THE LONG EIGHT

To the tune of "Haste to the Wedding"

PIPER'S FANCY

To the tune of "The New Rigged Ship"

DURHAM REEL

To the tune of "A Hundred Pipers"

JENNY PLUCK PEARS

Play 3 times

MAGE ON A CREE

Play 3 times (with repeat)

THE FINE COMPANION

Play 3 times

GATHERING PEASCODS

Play 3 times

PARSON'S FAREWELL

Play 3 times

HEY, BOYS, UP GO WE

Play 3 times

THE BLACK NAG

Play 3 times

NONESUCH
or
A LA MODE DE FRANCE

GODDESSES

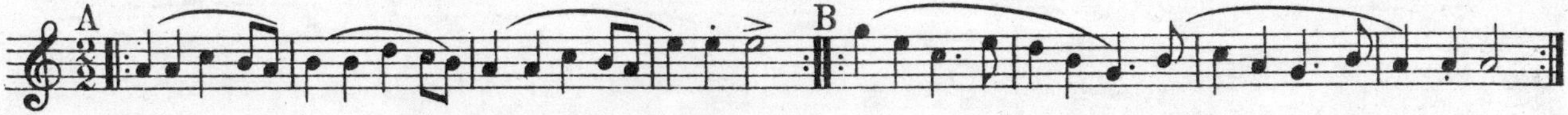

BLACK JACK

JAMAICA

IF ALL THE WORLD WERE PAPER

Play 12 times

HUNSDON HOUSE

Play 3 times

Play 4 times (i.e. 3 repeats)

CONFESS

Play 3 times

BROOM, THE BONNY, BONNY BROOM

Play 12 times

THE MERRY, MERRY MILKMAIDS

Play 3 times

OAKEN LEAVES

To the tune of "Touch and Take"

Play 18 times

PICKING UP STICKS

To the tune of "Lavena"

Play 17 times

SELLENGERS ROUND
or
THE BEGINNING OF THE WORLD

THE BOATMAN

SCOTCH CAP

CHRISTCHURCH BELLS

EPPING FOREST

THE MAID PEEPED OUT AT THE WINDOW
or
THE FRIAR IN THE WELL

CHILDGROVE

GREENWICH PARK

THE FIRST OF APRIL*

THE DRESSED SHIP*

*Published by kind permission of Mr. W.S. Porter

MELANCHOLY MARTIN

This tune can be used as an alternative accompaniment to the Hey in the Flamborough Sword Dance.

KIRKBY MALZEARD
(THE GIRL I LEFT BEHIND ME)

SLEIGHTS SWORD DANCE
Third Figure
THREE JOLLY SHEEPSKINS

Fourth Figure
BOYNE WATER

FLAMBOROUGH SWORD DANCE

THREE JOLLY SHEEPSKINS

HANDSWORTH SWORD DANCE

THE GIRL I LEFT BEHIND ME

ASKHAM RICHARD SWORD DANCE

THE FISHER LADDIE

ASKHAM RICHARD SWORD DANCE

BOBBY SHAFTOE

COUNTRY GARDENS

RIGS O' MARLOW

Introduction (4 bars). Then play 4 times.

TIDESWELL PROCESSIONAL MORRIS

Introduction (4 bars). Then repeat ad libitum.

BLUE-EYED STRANGER

Introduction (4 bars). Then play 4 times.

JOCKIE TO THE FAIR

Introduction (8 bars).

CONSTANT BILLY
ADDERBURY

Introduction (4 bars). Then play 6 times.

LADS A BUNCHUM
ADDERBURY

Introduction (8 bars). Then play 6 times.

GLORISHEARS
BAMPTON

Introduction (4 bars). Then play 3 times; and A music, a fourth time.

STEP BACK

Introduction (8 bars). Then play 3 times; and A music, a fourth time.

LADIES' PLEASURE

Introduction (8 bars). Then play A.B.C.B.C.B.

HELSTON FURRY DANCE

RECORDER METHODS

SOPRANO

H-117 Newman	"Recorder Playing in the Elementary School." A very easy school recorder book for beginners in the elementary schools. Choice solos and duets for Soprano Recorder, 3rd & 4th grades.	$1.00
H-125 Newman	"Recorder Playing for The Beginner." A very easy school recorder book for grades above the 4th and for Jr. High. Choice material	1.00
H-62 Newman	"The Hargail Melody Method: 'Music Around The Clock'" For Soprano Recorders. "This introductory method offers the beginner an excellent step by step plan of instruction covering the full tonal range of the instrument ... Excellent fingering diagrams ... A fine selection of folk tunes, selections from master composers and many old favorites ... "Dr. Wm. R. Sur, Chairman Music Education, Michigan State University. Correlated to "First Book of Duets" for Sopranos (H-64) and to "Easy Duets for Soprano-Alto Recorders." (H-65)	1.25
H-55 Burakoff	"The Elementary Method for the Soprano Recorder." Easy note at a time fingering progression. Range: low D to 4th line D. Correlated to "The Elementary Duet Book." (H-56).	1.25
Burakoff	"The Beginners Method for Soprano and Alto Recorder." A well planned easy instruction book with graded lessons for C and F recorders separately or in duet form. H-51 Part 1	1.75
	H-52 Part 2	1.95
H-60 Burakoff & Wheeler	"Music Making in the Elementary School" based on the concepts of Orff and Kodaly for Recorder, Voice, Bells and Rhythm instruments. Student's Edition	1.50
	H60-T Spiral Bound Teacher's Edition (with Lesson Plans)	3.95

ALTO

H-61 Newman	"The Hargail Melody Method" (Same as H-62) for Alto Recorders.	1.50
H-119 Newman	"Recorder Playing for The Beginner." An easy Alto method for use in schools and for adult beginners.	1.50
H-27 Dushkin	"Method for the Alto Recorder." A very easy beginner's book with folk tunes for one and two players.	.75

SOPRANO-ALTO

H-51 Burakoff	Part 1	"The Beginner's Method for Soprano and Alto Recorders."	1.75
H-52	Part 2	A well planned easy instruction book with graded lessons, for C and F recorders, individually or in duet form.	1.95

BASS

HRW-5 Gerboth & Prucha	"Primer for the Bass Recorder." Presented in both bass and treble clefs, with international folk-music; Loeillet, Woodcock, etc.	1.50